Other mini books in this series:
Love Quotations   Book Lover's Quotations
Friendship Quotations   Mother Quotations
Happiness Quotations   Business Quotations

Published in the USA in 1993 by Exley Giftbooks
Published in Great Britain in 1993 by Exley Publications Ltd
1st edition, 2nd printing 1993
1st edition, 3rd printing 1994
Copyright © Helen Exley 1993
Editor Helen Exley

ISBN 1-85015-308-6

A copy of the CIP data is available from the British
Library on request.

Selected by Helen Exley.
Designed by Pinpoint Design Company.
Pictures researched by Image Select.
Typesetting by Delta, Watford.
Printed and bound in Hungary.

Exley Publications Ltd, 16 Chalk Hill, Watford, Herts
WD1 4BN, United Kingdom.
Exley Giftbooks, 232 Madison Avenue, Suite 1206,
NY 10016, USA.

Exley Publications is very grateful to the following individuals and
organizations for permission to reproduce their pictures: Archiv Fur
Kunst, Berlin, cover and pages: 10/11, 12/13, 16/17, 22/23, 31, 34, 42;
Art Institute of Chicago, page 19; The Bridgeman Art Library, pages: 7,
20/21, 28, 32/33, 54, 55, 57; Mary Evans Picture Library, title page, page
53; Fine Art Photographic Library, page: 36; Giraudon, page 9; Museo
Chiossone, page 14; Musee d'Art Moderne, Paris, page 51; Musee des
Beaux-Arts, Tournai, page 57; Newlyn Orion Galleries, page 7; Scala,
pages: 14, 24, 26/27, 38/39, 40, 47, 48, 58/59; Prado, Madrid, page 48;
Royal Holloway and Bedford New College, pages: 20/21, 32/33;
Telegraph Colour Library, page 45.

THE BEST OF
WOMEN'S
QUOTATIONS

EDITED BY
HELEN EXLEY

EXLEY
NEW YORK • WATFORD, UK

"I want to be all that I am capable of becoming...."
KATHERINE MANSFIELD (1888 - 1923)

"I believe that we are solely responsible for our choices, and we have to accept the consequences of every deed, word, and thought throughout our lifetime."
ELISABETH KÜBLER-ROSS, b.1926

"My will shall shape my future. Whether I fail or succeed shall be no man's doing but my own. I am the force; I can clear any obstacle before me or I can be lost in the maze. My choice; my responsibility; win or lose, only I hold the key to my destiny."
ELAINE MAXWELL

"I say if it's going to be done, let's do it. Let's not put it in the hands of fate. Let's not put it in the hands of someone who doesn't know me. I know me best. Then take a breath and go ahead."
ANITA BAKER

"Challenges make you discover
things about yourself that you never
really knew. They're what make the
instrument stretch - what make you
go beyond the norm."
CICELY TYSON

"You gain strength, courage and
confidence by every experience which you
must stop and look fear in the face...
You must do the thing you think
you cannot do."
ELEANOR ROOSEVELT (1884 - 1962)

"I have always grown from my
problems and challenges, from the
things that don't work out, that's when
I've really learned."
CAROL BURNETT, b.1936

"I own my life. And only mine. And so I
shall appreciate my person. And so I shall
make proper use of myself."
RUTH BEEBE HILL, b.1913

"Women have always been the
guardians of wisdom and humanity
which makes them natural, but
usually secret, rulers.

The time has come for them to rule openly, but together with and not against men."

CHARLOTTE WOLFF (1904 - 1986)

"We do as much, we eat as much, we want as much."
SOJOURNER TRUTH (1777 - 1883)

"The prolonged slavery of women is the darkest page in human history."
ELIZABETH STANTON (1815 - 1902)

"Women constitute half the world's population, perform nearly two-thirds of its work hours, receive one-tenth of the world's income and own less than one-hundredth of the world's property."

UNITED NATIONS REPORT, 1980

"The cock croweth but the hen delivereth
the goods."
ANONYMOUS

"Woman's work! Housework's the hardest
work in the world.
That's why men won't do it."
EDNA FERBER (1887 - 1968)

"Women are expected to do twice
as much as men in half the time and for
no credit. Fortunately this
isn't difficult."
CHARLOTTE WHITTON (1896 - 1975)

"Women speak because they wish to speak, whereas a man speaks only when driven to speech by something outside himself - like, for instance, he can't find any clean socks."

JEAN KERR, b.1923

"I refuse to consign the whole male sex to the nursery. I insist on believing that some men are my equals."

BRIGID BROPHY

"Women have served all these centuries as looking glasses possessing the ... power of reflecting the figure of man at twice its natural size."

VIRGINIA WOOLF (1882 - 1941)

"I'm furious about the Women's Liberationists. They keep getting up on soapboxes and proclaiming that women are brighter than men. That's true, but it should be kept very quiet or it ruins the whole racket."

ANITA LOOS (1888 - 1981)

"Women will always fear war more than men because they are mothers. A woman will always have a baby, her own or her children's in her arms. She will always be tormented by fear for her children, the fear that one day she might be a witness to their own deaths."

NATALYA BARANSKAYA

"Arise, all women who have hearts,
whether your baptism be that of water or
tears! Say firmly 'We will not have great
questions decided by irrelevant agencies....
We ... will be too tender of those of another
country to allow our sons to be trained to
injure theirs.' "

JULIA WARD HOWE (1819 - 1910)

"At a birth the heavens lean down,
or perhaps it is that the racked body is
spun fine to be aware of eternal things -
we women hardly know how lucky
we are in this."

KATHERINE TREVELYAN

"Of all the joys that lighten suffering
earth, what joy is welcomed like
a new-born child?"

CAROLINE NORTON (1808 - 1877)

"Making the decision to have a child -
it's momentous. It is to decide forever to
have your heart go walking around outside
your body."

ELIZABETH STONE

"Women's liberation is just a lot
of foolishness. It's the men
who are discriminated against.
They can't bear children. And
no one's likely to do
anything about that."

GOLDA MEIR (1898 - 1978)

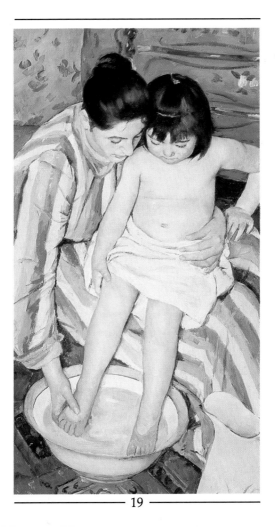

"The world has never yet seen a truly great
and virtuous nation, because in the
degradation of woman the very fountains
of life are poisoned at their source."

LUCRETIA MOTT (1793 - 1880)
speaking at the first Women's Rights Convention, 1848

"Rape is ... nothing more or less than
a conscious process of intimidation
by which all men keep all women in a
state of fear."

SUSAN BROWNMILLER, b.1935,
from "Against Our Will"

"Women as a class have never subjugated another group; we have never marched off to wars of conquest in the name of the fatherland.
We have never been involved in a decision to annex the territory of a neighboring country, or to fight for foreign markets on distant shores.
These are the games men play, not us.
We want to be neither oppressors nor oppressed.
The women's revolution is the final revolution of them all."

SUSAN BROWNMILLER, b.1935,
from "Sisterhood is Powerful" in the "New York Times", March 15, 1970

"Why we oppose votes for men ... because men are too emotional to vote. Their conduct at baseball games and political conventions shows this, while their innate tendency to appeal to force renders them particularly unfit for the task of government."

ALICE DUER MILLER (1874 - 1942)

"Women are the only exploited group in history who have been idealized into powerlessness."

ERICA JONG, b.1942

"Mother as an ideal is unfair in the same manner as woman as a sex object."

LIZ SMITH
from "The Mother Book"

"The sentimental cult of domestic virtues is the cheapest method at society's disposal of keeping women quiet without seriously considering their grievances or improving their position."

ALVA MYRDAL and VIOLA KLEIN,
from "Women's Two Roles"

"I don't like the terms 'housewife' and 'homemaker'. I prefer to be called 'Domestic Goddess'... it's more descriptive."

ROSEANNE BARR

They talk about a woman's sphere as
though it had a limit;
There's not a place in earth or heaven,
There's not a task to mankind given,
There's not a blessing or a woe,

There's not a whispered 'yes' or 'no',
There's not a life, or death, or birth,
That has a feather's weight of worth
Without a woman in it.

KATE FIELD (1838 - 1896)

"It is vain to say human beings ought to be satisfied with tranquillity: they must have action; and they will make it if they cannot find it. Millions are condemned to a stiller doom than mine, and millions are in silent revolt against their lot. Nobody knows how many rebellions besides political rebellions ferment.... Women are supposed to be very calm generally. But women feel just as men feel: they need exercise for their faculties, and a field for their efforts, as much as their brothers do; they suffer from too rigid a restraint, too absolute a stagnation, precisely as men would suffer; and it is narrow-minded in their more privileged fellow-creatures to say that they ought to confine themselves to making puddings and knitting stockings, to playing on the piano and embroidering bags. It is thoughtless to condemn them, or laugh at them, if they seek to do more or learn more than custom has pronounced necessary for their sex."

CHARLOTTE BRONTË (1816 - 1855),
from "Jane Eyre"

"Because of their agelong training in human relations - for that is what feminine intuition really is - women have a special contribution to make to any group enterprise...."

MARGARET MEAD (1901 - 1978)

"Women have a way of treating people more softly. We treat souls with kid gloves."

SHIRLEY CAESAR

"Women are repeatedly accused of taking things personally. I cannot see any other honest way of taking them."

MARYA MANNES, b.1904

"What is truly indispensible for the conduct of life has been taught us by women - the small rules of courtesy, the actions that win us the warmth or deference of others; the words that assure us a welcome; the attitudes that must be varied to mesh with character or situation; all social strategy. It is listening to women that teaches us to speak to men."

R. DE GOURMONT (1858 - 1915)

"I've got a woman's ability to stick to a job and get on with it when everyone else walks off and leaves it."

MARGARET THATCHER, b. 1925

"If a woman is sufficiently ambitious, determined *and* gifted - there is practically nothing she can't do."

HELEN LAWRENSON (1904 - 1982)

"The especial genius of women I believe to be electrical in movement, intuitive in function, spiritual in tendency."
MARGARET FULLER (1810 - 1850)

"All women hustle. Women watch faces, voices, gestures, moods.... She's the person who has to survive through cunning."
MARGE PIERCY, b.1936

"A woman has to be twice as good as a man to go half as far."
FANNIE HURST (1889 - 1968)

"I would venture to guess that Anon, who wrote so many poems without signing them, was often a woman."
VIRGINIA WOOLF (1882 - 1941)

"Nobody objects to a woman being a good writer or sculptor or geneticist if at the same time she manages to be a good wife, good mother, good looking, good tempered, well groomed and unaggressive."
LESLIE M. MCINTYRE

"When a man gets up to speak, people listen then look.
When a woman gets up, people look; then, if they like what they see, they listen."
PAULINE FREDERICK (1883 - 1938)

"Once you live with the issue of women
and the landscape for a while, you
find that you cannot separate them from
the notions of peace, spirituality, and
community. As women we must learn
to become leaders in society, not just for
our own sake, but for the sake of all
people. We must support and protect
our kinship with the environment
for the generations to come."

CHINA GALLAND

"Erotic comes from the Greek word eros,
the personification of love in all its
aspects ... and personifying creative power
and harmony. When I speak of the
erotic, then, I speak of it as an assertion
of the life force of women, of that
creative energy empowered, the
knowledge and use of which we are
now reclaiming in our language, our
history, our dancing, our loving,
our work, our lives."

AUDRE LORDE, b.1934

"The dogma of woman's complete
historical subjection to man
must be rated as one of the most
fantastic myths ever created by the
human mind."

MARY RITTER BEARD (1876 - 1958)

"I myself have never been able to find out
precisely what feminism is: I only know
that people call me a feminist whenever I
express sentiments that differentiate me
from a doormat."

REBECCA WEST (1892 - 1983)

"When we take away the right to an individual name, we symbolically take away the right to be an individual. Immigration officials did this to refugees, husbands routinely do it to wives."

ERICA JONG, b.1942

"Dear Sirs, man to man, manpower, craftsman, working men, the thinking man, the man in the street, fellow countrymen, the history of mankind, one-man show, man in his wisdom, statesman, forefathers, masterful, masterpiece, old masters, the brotherhood of man, Liberty, Equality, Fraternity, sons of free men, faith of our fathers, god the father, god the son, yours fraternally, amen.
Words fail me."

STEPHANIE DOWRICK

"Declaration of Sentiments:...We hold these truths to be self-evident: that all men and women are created equal..."

ELIZABETH STANTON (1815 - 1902)

"If civilization is to advance at all in the future, it must be through the help of women, women freed of their political shackles, women with full power to work their will in society."

EMMELINE PANKHURST (1857 - 1928)

"Why, then, do women need power? *Because power is freedom.* Power allows us to accomplish what is important to us, in the manner that we best see fit. It separates the doers from the dreamers."

PATTI F. MANCINI, *in a speech, 1989*

"In education, in marriage, in religion, in everything, disappointment is the lot of women. It shall be the business of my life to deepen this disappointment in every woman's heart until she bows down to it no longer."

LUCY STONE (1818 - 1893)

"I'm not denying that women are foolish. God Almighty made them to match men."

GEORGE ELIOT (MARY ANN EVANS) (1819 - 1880)

"The great and almost only comfort about being a woman is that one can always pretend to be more stupid than one is and no one is surprised."

FREYA STARK, b.1893

"The average girl would rather have beauty than brains because she knows that the average man can see much better than he can think."

"LADIES HOME JOURNAL", 1947

"In passing, also, I would like to say that the first time Adam had a chance he laid the blame on woman."

NANCY ASTOR (1879 - 1964)

"I require only three things in a man: he must be handsome, ruthless and stupid."

DOROTHY PARKER (1893 - 1967)

"The hardest task in a girl's life is to prove to a man that his intentions are serious."

HELEN ROWLAND (1875 - 1950)

"When he is late for dinner and I know he must be either having an affair or lying dead in the street, I always hope he's dead."

JUDITH VIORST, b.1931

"I don't believe man is woman's natural enemy. Perhaps his lawyer is."

SHANA ALEXANDER, b.1925

"It's as if women are in a totally rigged race. A lot of men are driving souped-up, low-slung racing cars and we're running as fast as we can in tennis shoes we managed to salvage from a local garage sale."

NAOMI WEISSTEIN, b.1939

"Woman: the peg on which the wit hangs his jest, the preacher his text, the cynic his grouch and the sinner his justification."

HELEN ROWLAND (1876 - 1950)

"It occurred to me when I was thirteen and wearing white gloves and Mary Janes and going to dancing school, that no one should have to dance backward all their lives."

JILL RUCKELSHAUS, b.1937

"The women's position in the world today is so much harder than a man's that it makes me choke every time I hear a man complain about *anything!*"

KATHARINE HEPBURN, b.1909

"Become a true expert in something.
Anything. Then the question of you being
a woman will barely raise its head."
DR. JANINE COOPER

"No one can make you feel inferior
without your own consent."
ELEANOR ROOSEVELT (1884 - 1962)

"We're swallowed up only when we are
willing for it to happen."
NATHALIE SARRAUTE, b.1900

"Never grow a wishbone,
daughter, where your backbone
ought to be."
CLEMENTINE PADDLEFORD (1900 - 1968)

"You have got to discover you, what you
do, and trust it."
BARBRA STREISAND, b.1942

"Don't compromise yourself. You're all
you've got."
JANIS JOPLIN (1943 - 1970)

"Growing up female in America. What a
liability! You grew up with your ears full
of cosmetic ads, love songs, advice
columns, whoreoscopes, Hollywood
gossip, and moral dilemmas on the level of
TV soap operas. What litanies the
advertisers of the good life chanted at you!
What curious catechisms!"

ERICA JONG, b.1942

"Above all, remember that the most
important thing you can take anywhere is
not a Gucci bag or French-cut jeans; it's an
open mind."
GAIL RUBIN BERENY

"Taking joy in life is a woman's
best cosmetic."
ROSALIND RUSSELL (1911 - 1976)

"You have to admit that most
women who have done something
with their lives have been disliked by
almost everyone."
FRANCOISE GILOT

"The men who espoused unpopular causes
may have been considered misguided, but
they were rarely attacked for their morals
or their masculinity.
Women who did the same thing
were apt to be denounced as
harlots or condemned for being
unfeminine - an all-purpose word that was
used to describe almost any category of
female behavior of which men
disapproved."
MARGARET TRUMAN, b.1924

"To think that all in me of which
my father would have felt proper
pride had I been a man, is
deeply mortifying to him because
I am a woman."
ELIZABETH CADY STANTON (1815 - 1902)

"Imagination is the highest kite
one can fly."
LAUREN BACALL, b.1924

"Risk! Risk anything! Care no more for the
opinions of others, for those voices. Do the
hardest thing on earth for you. Act for
yourself. Face the truth."
KATHERINE MANSFIELD (1888 - 1923)

"If you play it safe in life you've
decided that you don't want to
grow any more."
SHIRLEY HUFSTEDLER, b.1925

"Supposing you have tried and failed
again and again. You may have a fresh
start any moment you choose, for this thing
that we call 'failure' is not the falling down,
but the staying down."
MARY PICKFORD (1893 - 1979)

"If I had to live my life over again, I'd dare
to make more mistakes next time."
NADINE STAIR

"Now, as always, the most
automated appliance in a household
is the mother."
BEVERLY JONES, b.1927

"I am a source of satisfaction to him, a
nurse, a piece of furniture, a *woman* -
nothing more."
SOPHIE TOLSTOY (1844 - 1919)

"I believe that what woman resents is not so much giving herself in pieces as giving herself purposelessly."

ANNE MORROW LINDBERGH, b.1906

"Woman will always be dependent until she holds a purse of her own."

ELIZABETH CADY STANTON (1815 - 1902)

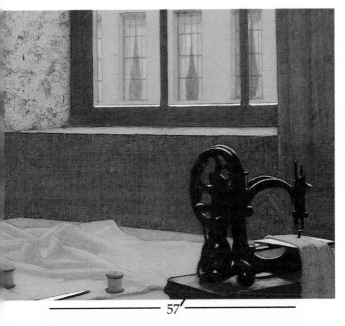

"Please know that I am aware of the hazards. I want to do it because I want to do it. Women must try to do things as men have tried. When they fail, their failure must be but a challenge to others."

AMELIA EARHART (1898 - 1937),
in a letter to her husband, before her last flight

"The state of the world today demands that women become less modest and dream/plan/act/risk on a larger scale."

CHARLOTTE BUNCH, b.1944

"It is ridiculous to take on a man's job just in order to be able to say that 'a woman has done it - yah!' The only decent reason for tackling a job is that it is *your* job, and *you* want to do it."

DOROTHY SAYERS (1893 - 1957),
from "Are Women Human?"

"A liberated woman is one who feels confident in herself, and is happy in what she is doing. She is a person who has a sense of self...It all comes down to freedom of choice."

BETTY FORD, b.1939

Yes, I am wise, but it's wisdom full of pain
Yes, I've paid the price, but look how much
I've gained
I am wise, I am invincible, I am Woman.

HELEN REDDY, b.1941,
From the song, "I Am Woman"

"The fact is, I can have any experience of life I want. I don't have to choose any one thing or act in any one way to define myself as a woman now. I am one."

ALLY SHEEDY, b.1962